Easy Strateg
People Of Tl
You!

Mean People

Meditation, Mindfulness, And Other Strategies To Increase Emotional Intelligence, Peace Of Mind, And Self Esteem!

Ryan Cooper

STOP!!! Before you read any further....Would you like to know the Secrets of Transforming your life, overcome insecurities, develop leadership skills, and undeniable confidence in your personal, professional, and relationship life?

If your answer is yes, then you are not alone. Thousands of people are looking for the secret to have unstoppable confidence and self-driven power in all areas of their lives.

If you have been searching for these answers without much luck, you're in the right place!

Not only will you gain incredible insight in this book, but because I want to make sure to give you as much value as possible, right now for a limited time you can get full **100% FREE access to a VIP bonus EBook** entitled **LIMITLESS ENERGY!**

<u>**Just Go Here For Free Instant Access:**</u>

<u>www.PotentialRise.com</u>

Legal Notice

Disclaimer Notice

Table Of Contents

Introduction

I want to thank you and congratulate you for purchasing the book, *"Mean People: Easy Strategies To Rob Mean People Of Their Power Over You! - Meditation, Mindfulness, And Other Strategies To Increase Emotional Intelligence, Peace Of Mind, And Self Esteem!"*.

Mean People Won't Have Any Control Over You Anymore!

This "Mean People" book contains proven steps and strategies on how to understand the psychology of mean people, and better yet, how you can either help to change them, or if changing them is out of the question, how you can emotionally remove any power they have over you!

This book also contains helpful information on how you can confront mean people without compromising your job or personal life. Here, you will find tips on how to deal with difficult people in your workplace as well as how to achieve inner peace within five minutes before confrontation.

Moreover, this book contains useful advice on how to deal with jealous people and their mean antics. You will find out how you can effectively overcome your fear of confrontation and stand up to mean people. In this book, you will also read about using meditation and mindfulness to get better control of your emotions.

Thanks again for purchasing this book, I hope you enjoy it!

Chapter 1: Understanding The Psychology Behind Mean People – Why Are They Most Likely So Mean?

Every person is unique in his own way. No two people have exactly the same characteristics or personality. There are plenty of nice people in the world; but sadly, there are also a lot of mean people. Why are there mean people, anyway? What has made them act and speak the way they do?

Well, it is quite easy to figure out the motivations of people getting along with others. Humans are social beings that need to have positive relationships. Society will not exist if people do not get along and cooperate with one another. Nevertheless, some people stay mean due to a number of reasons.

Positive distinctiveness, for instance, is one reason why some people are mean. According to the social identity theory, humans have a psychological need for positive distinctiveness. This means that they need to feel unique from other people in a positive manner. Such need extends to groups that they belong to.

Individuals tend to view their in-groups better than their out-groups. They display favoritism towards the members of their group. Because of this, people who are not part of the group are perceived as outcasts and not treated very well. This is especially true when they seem to challenge the identity of others.

According to researchers, individuals tend to boost their self-esteem when they are able to degrade people that are not part of their group. Conversely, the social comparison theory states that it is natural for people to compare themselves with other people. Such comparisons can either make them feel better or worse about themselves.

Because humans generally want to feel good, they become prone to making downward comparisons. They look down on other people to feel better about themselves and boost their own self-esteem. Researchers also state that people become more negative towards their peers when they have been belittled or insulted.

According to a study that involved people being given fake feedback, people are more likely to demean others when they are insulted. In this study, a group of individuals were told they were unattractive while another group was told that they were attractive. The group who thought that they were unattractive rated others as less intelligent, less kind, and less attractive.

Classical projection is another possible reason why people are mean. According to Sigmund Freud, a neurologist who discovered psychoanalysis, people tend to cope with their negative views about themselves by thinking that other people are worse than they are. For instance, if you feel dishonest, you may think that other people are more dishonest. Because of this, you will immediately feel better that someone is worse than you.

Furthermore, mean people may act the way they do because they feel that their egos are being threatened. Researchers have found that a threatened self-esteem can drive so much aggression. So it does not really matter if a person feels bad or good about himself in general.

What truly matters is that that person feels worse about himself than usual at that exact moment. Researchers have also proven that a threatened self-esteem can lead to aggressive behaviors. An example of this is when a person becomes insulted, he becomes likely to act obnoxious towards another.

So in conclusion, a person becomes mean in order to promote himself or his group. He becomes more aggressive when his self-worth is challenged or when he does not feel good about himself. He becomes more likely to compare himself with other people when his self-esteem is threatened.

He views other people as being worse or having more negative traits in order to feel better. He also degrades people who he perceives are not members of his group. Basically, insecurity is the root of meanness. When a person criticizes or insults someone, it may actually say more about himself than the other person.

Chapter 2: Can You Help To Change These Difficult People And Make Them Not Act Mean Anymore?

People often try to change other people in the hopes of making them better. Sadly, one cannot change someone who is not willing. So no matter how good your intentions are, you still cannot change someone who does not want to change on his own. You cannot make a difficult person not act mean anymore unless that person is willing to do so.

A lot of people have this notion that they cannot change. They believe that it is who they are. However, this is not true because people can change. You may be a creature of habit, but your personality is not in your DNA. You can change the way you speak and act, but it will take time and effort.

Why is it difficult for people to change? Well, people tend to have a hard time changing themselves even if they genuinely want to do so because of the patterns and habits that they have been used to. When you have been doing something for so many years or ever since you can remember, it will be really hard to get out of that pattern.

For instance, you can tell someone that he is fat and that he should no longer eat fast food. However, telling that person does not guarantee that he will no longer eat fast food. People do not behave badly because they are lacking information regarding their shortcomings.

People behave badly because they have fallen into destructive behavioral patterns from which they are not able to escape. The behavior of humans calls for constant prodding and not blunt hectoring. So if you want to get a person out of his negative cascade, you should not attack his bad behavior.

Instead, you should go on the offense and focus on alternative good behaviors. Some researchers even suggest that you obliquely tackle negative behavior by redirecting your attention towards positive ones. It is also best to focus on one area at a time rather than change everything all at once.

If you really want to help a person change his ways, you should make him aware of his behavior. Awareness is the first process towards change. Go ahead and confront the mean person. Be objective and let him know about his behavior. Tell that person how his attitude makes an impact on you and others, but do not be pushy.

If this person realizes what he is doing, then he would be inclined to change. On the other hand, if he still thinks that he is not doing anything wrong, then that is no longer your problem. You can encourage people to change for the better, but you cannot make them change. It is up to them if they will change or not.

Chapter 3: How To Emotionally Deal With Scenarios Where You Cannot Change The Mean People

As you have learned from the previous chapter, you cannot have control over other people's behavior. Yes, you can try to help and encourage them to change. However, no matter what you do or how hard you try, the ultimate decision is still theirs. Even if your intentions are good and genuine, you will still not be able to change a person who is not completely willing to change.

So how should you act in situations in which you are forced to deal with difficult people? Well, first of all, you should stay grounded. Be confident and secure with yourself. Always remember your worth as a person. You should stay intact no matter how many times other people try to bring you down. Being confident and secure with yourself will enable you to handle difficult situations with class and poise.

Always be polite and rational even if the other person is being a jerk. Do not stoop down to his level by talking and acting the same way. It is best to avoid mean people, but if you must deal with them, you should do your best to keep cool. Never lose your temper and always be careful with the words that come out of your mouth.

Likewise, you should resist the urge to assume or judge. Yes, it can be difficult to show someone compassion when you think that you have them pegged. However, even though it may seem unlikely for that person to change, you still have to believe that it is possible. People can actually change.

Also, if you harbor negative thoughts, they tend to come out in your body language. This may make other people tempted to mirror your negativity. So, you should try to come at them with a positive mindset that you wish they have. You should expect the best in these people for you can never tell when a pleasant surprise might come.

Another good advice that you need to follow is to understand where mean people come from. Sometimes, a person acts mean because this is his way of crying out for help. So before you judge someone, see to it that you understand why they behave that way. Approach people like these with firmness and kindness so they do not bring you down.

You also have to maintain a positive boundary. When you interact with a mean person, you should protect your positive space. If the negativity of that person is so strong, you should just try to walk away. Help mean people feel more positive about themselves instead of nagging them to act more positive.

What if the mean people are members of your family? Well, in this case, it may not be possible to simply walk away and cut ties with them. So in order for you to be able to hold onto your peace, you should try talking to them. If they will not listen, just try to avoid long term interactions with them, such as during reunions, weddings, etc.

Stay respectful, but do not let them drag you down. If you want to feel good, you should not surround yourself with negative people. They are your family, so you should respect them. However, this does not give them the right to bully you or make you feel bad about yourself. You should learn how to be mature when controlling your emotions.

Chapter 4: Rob Mean People Of Their Power Over You By Adopting Meditation And Gaining Greater Peace Of Mind

Meditation is a great way to calm your mind and relax your body. When you are feeling a little weary, just sit back and meditate. You can meditate anytime and anywhere. You can meditate in a spare room in your home, in your garden, in a temple, or in the mountains. The key to meditating is silence and concentration.

Meditating every once in a while can keep your mind and body healthy. This is especially true if you have a very busy lifestyle and a crazy schedule. If you frequently deal with people with various behaviors, you can be stressed and this can have a negative impact on your health.

Meditating trains you to control your emotions better. It also gives you time to focus and analyze your behavior and attitude towards other people. When you meditate, you are able to realize things that you may have not realized before. Meditating gives you more awareness of your thoughts and actions.

Also, meditating lets you release anger, frustration, and anxiety. If you encounter a mean person, you should never respond with negativity. Always counteract negativity with positivity. If you meditate on a regular basis, you will be able to master the mindfulness techniques that will enable you to become a more positive individual.

If you show kindness to a mean person, that person may be prompted to think of his actions towards you. You may also inspire him to change since he will feel that you are compassionate and understanding towards his meanness. Once again, meanness can signify a cry for help. So, you should not immediately judge people who are mean.

Mean people are usually full of insecurities. They act mean towards others when they feel threatened. They become mean to hide their true emotions and to show that they are confident. They bully and belittle other people because they want to feel better about themselves. Being mean tends to make them feel stronger, wiser, and generally better.

By being kind and compassionate towards mean people, you will rob them of their power. They will be puzzled as to why you are acting that way instead of feeling scared and helpless. They will not have control over your emotions because you do not feel threatened of them.

You should just ignore mean comments and remarks if you know that those are not true. When you are not threatened, you are able to achieve peace of mind. When you are secure with yourself, you do not feel the need to fight against mean people because that is just a waste of your precious time.

Chapter 5: How To Use Mindfulness And Meditation Strategies To Control Your Own Emotions

Controlling your emotions can be pretty hard, especially if you are a hot-tempered person. However, controlling your emotions is possible and actually rewarding. If you take charge of your emotions instead of letting your emotions take over your life, you will be happier and more peaceful.

So how can you gain better control of your emotions? Well, you can practice meditation and mindfulness techniques. As you have learned from the previous chapter, meditation can improve your mind and body. Meditation is good for your mental, physical, and spiritual health.

Once in a while, you should get in touch with your spiritual and emotional self. It is not enough to just take care of your physical health. Eating nutritious foods and exercising on a regular basis do not suffice. You also need to relax your mind and improve your emotional well-being.

If you practice meditation and mindfulness on a regular basis, you will be able to train your mind to be more rational and peaceful. When you meditate, you are able to focus on your train of thoughts. You can think about the things that usually agitate you and how you often react to the comments of other people towards you.

Evaluate yourself and your reactions towards mean people. Were you able to keep your cool when confronted by a bully co-worker? Were you able to stay respectful with relatives who kept making sarcastic remarks about your job and relationship status? Were you able to stay calm around people who constantly comment about your looks?

Remember the times when people commented negatively towards your appearance, job, place of living, etc. If you still get angry upon recalling such incidents, then you have not yet fully moved on. Even if those events were already in the past and those people may no longer contact you, they still remain in your life because they still affect you.

Allow yourself to move on from these negative experiences so you can grow as a person. Maturity does not come with age, but with experience and self-realizations. You should free yourself from past anger, hurt, and frustrations. Instead, focus on the present and what you can do to have a better future.

Do not let the people who are mean to you bring you down. More importantly, do not let the thoughts of people who were mean to you still affect you. Remember them and what they did; but rather than dwelling on the past, forgive them and let go. It is difficult to carry a grudge towards others, so just let go and live a stress-free life.

Chapter 6: What Is Emotional Intelligence And How Can It Help You To Dealing With Difficult And Mean People?

Your ability to control and express your emotions is important. However, you should realize that your ability to understand, interpret, and respond to the emotions of other people is important too. Also, while being good with academics can take you places, being emotionally intelligent may be more important.

Emotional intelligence is the ability to control, evaluate, and perceive emotions. Some experts suggest that it is actually more important than IQ. Some researchers also believe that emotional intelligence can be strengthened and learned, while others state that it is an inborn characteristic. Anyway, there are four branches of emotional intelligence.

These four branches are perceiving emotions, reasoning with emotions, understanding emotions, and managing emotions. Perceiving emotions is your first step towards understanding them. This may involve understanding body language, facial expressions, and other nonverbal signals.

Reasoning with emotions is the second branch. This involves making use of emotions to promote cognitive activity and thinking. Your emotions help you prioritize things. You tend to respond emotionally towards things that get your attention.

The third branch is about understanding your emotions. Take note that the emotions you perceive can have different meanings. If a person expresses an angry emotion, an observer should interpret the cause of this anger and what it can mean. For instance, if your boss seems angry, he may not be satisfied with your work or he has a personal issue. There can actually be a number of reasons as to why he might be angry.

Finally, there is managing emotions. Your ability to manage your emotions is a vital part of your emotional intelligence. Other important aspects of emotional management include regulating emotions, responding to the emotions of other people, and responding appropriately to emotions.

You can say that you are emotionally intelligent if you can control your emotions well. This is when you do not get angry easily and you are able to rationalize things before making a reaction. Emotionally intelligent people do not easily become affected or threatened with the opinions and actions of the people around them.

Hence, individuals who want to be able to deal with difficult and mean people better should work on their emotional intelligence. You need to improve the way you perceive, understand, and respond to the remarks or actions of other people. If you are secure with yourself, you will be able to handle sticky situations gracefully.

Chapter 7: How To Overcome Fear Of Mean People, Be Confident, And Stand Up To Them

First of all, you have to realize that you are a unique person who is capable of doing so many wonderful things. You may not think that you are smart if you often fail in school. However, you should realize that grades are not the sole basis for intelligence. You may not do well in class, but you can be great at sports, art, dancing, etc. You are an amazing individual, which is why you should not be overly conscious with what other people say.

Likewise, if your boss often belittles your skills or your co-workers frequently poke fun at you, you should realize that you may not really be the problem. If you know that you are doing your best at work, you should not doubt yourself. Your boss could be acting mean because he is threatened that you may get ahead of him or your co-workers are simply jealous of your skills.

If you are true to yourself and you try hard to accomplish your goals, other people can see you as a threat to their own security. They become mean towards you because they want to eliminate you, so they will no longer feel threatened. They can also be mean because they want you to feel bad about yourself, so you will not be able to function at your best. Whatever the reason is, you should not let mean people get the best of you.

The world is full of difficult and mean people. This is just inevitable. Every day, you will be exposed to people with varying attitudes and behaviors. However, it is not really what they do or say that matters but rather the way you react towards them. They can try to make you feel inferior, but if you are secured with your own value, nothing they do will make you have a bad day.

It is a matter of self-esteem, really. If you are confident, you will not even realize that people are being mean towards you. You will just brush off nasty comments or insensitive remarks. On the other hand, if you are the type of person who is meek or shy, then it is high time that you work on your personality. If you do not change your ways, people will always try to undermine you.

You can always try self-help as your primary option. You can buy self-help books or download videos and audios online. You can also read articles about tips on how to boost your self-esteem. Follow the advice of experts and do not be afraid of rejection. You can also seek a therapist to help you out. Getting professional advice is ideal, so you will be able to think things through more thoroughly.

If people often make nasty remarks about your figure, the way you walk, or the way you talk, you can enroll in a workshop or get a gym membership. Improving your posture and diction can significantly boost your confidence. Likewise, looking good by losing weight and toning your body can make you feel better about yourself. If you look good, you will feel good.

When a mean person comes up to you and tries to bring you down, you can either walk away or answer back. Sometimes, ignoring the bully and simply walking away is advisable; but when that person crosses the line, you may need to stand up to him. When confronting a difficult person, make sure that you are calm and objective. Do not aggravate the situation by using profanities or rude gestures.

Do not be afraid of mean people because you are better than them. You know that you are better than them because you are emotionally secured and you do not feel the need to lash out on others in order to feel good about yourself. Mean people are often insecure and in need of attention. They also act mean towards others in order to show that they are confident, cool, witty, etc. even when they are not.

You can also ask the mean person what his problem is and if there is anything you can do to help him out. Oftentimes, difficult and mean people just need someone who can understand them. They may be going through something and lashing out on you is not really personal. They may need help, so you should be compassionate towards them instead of immediately judging them.

Chapter 8: Dealing With Jealousy And Knowing If It Is The Source For People Acting So Mean

A jealous person can act mean in order to defend his territory. This can be evident in the workplace, in relationships, and even in homes. There can be various incidents that display jealousy. At home, one of your siblings can be mean towards you if you did something good and your parents applaud you for it. At the office, one of your co-workers can be jealous if your boss rewards you for a job well done. In a relationship, your partner might feel threatened when someone else gets your attention.

Although jealousy is bad, it is an emotion that people experience naturally. Jealousy can have both positive and negative consequences. A jealous person can use his jealousy to motivate himself to do better next time, for instance. On the other hand, jealousy can also drive people to act negative towards other people. So if someone becomes jealous of your appearance, intelligence, or skills, he can be mean towards you.

What can you do in situations like this and how can you know if jealousy is the reason why people are acting so mean? Well, in all situations, you should try your best to stay calm and rational. Do not be defensive and start calling people out. You have to be relaxed, so you can think of the most appropriate move. Every reaction you make can either have a positive or negative consequence, so you need to be very careful.

Anyway, if you know that you are civil or friendly to everyone and that you are putting all your efforts in what you do, then the problem is not with you when someone becomes mean towards you. You have to understand that it is common for jealous people to act the way they do because they are actually afraid of you. So before you realize that you actually have power over them, they try to destroy your confidence and get rid of you.

If you get in a conflict with a mean or difficult person, you can use the Detach, Disassociate, and Diffuse strategy. First, you should detach by remaining calm in the midst of a heated argument or confrontation. This is crucial for your personal preservation. You should never let out any profanities, rude gestures, or extreme emotions to prevent the stimulation of more difficult behavior from the other person.

You can also choose to disassociate or remove yourself from that situation. Just be indifferent and do not mind the mean person. Also, you should never talk about that person in his face or behind his back. If you do, you will just allow yourself to go down to his level. So instead of doing this, you should focus on something else. Just forget about that mean person. After all, he is not really that important in your life.

Finally, you can choose to diffuse. You should realize that the truthful party usually wins the confrontation or argument. So you should start asking why and try to move your conversation to a higher level. If you know that you are in the right, you should not be afraid or hesitant. Oftentimes, mean people only appear tough. In reality, they are actually afraid of what you are capable of.

Chapter 9: What To Do If The Mean People Are Coworkers

Dealing with difficult people in the workplace can be very easier said than done. You have to see and interact with them every day and if you have signed a contract with the company, you may not be able to resign as soon as you want. So what can you do to have peace of mind at work?

Well, see to it that you still perform at your optimum level no matter how nasty your coworkers are. If you are good and your boss recognizes your efforts, your coworkers can feel threatened, thus prompting them to bully you in order to destroy your self-esteem.

When your coworkers undermine you, you should realize that it is not you who has the problem. The problem is actually with them because they are insecure, incompetent, and jealous. Keep in mind that you are a mature adult who can handle things in a reasonable manner. Always keep your cool and create backup plans.

First, you can try to ignore your mean coworkers. When they gossip about you within your earshot, just ignore them and continue on doing your work. After all, people who truly know you will not easily believe malicious gossips and hearsays. Simply let the issue fade out naturally.

If your mean coworker keeps bothering you while you work, tell him about it. It is more ideal to confront that person in private so as not to attract unwanted attention that might embarrass him and make him act meaner towards you. Confronting a difficult person can be hard, but it has to be done.

Also, remember that mean people are only effective when they are on solid ground that you can take away. You should not tolerate the bad behavior of a coworker. If you give in, be prepared to expect more. Tell your mean coworker that if he does not stop his unprofessional antics, you will tell about it to your employer or the human resources.

If your mean coworker bullies you on a regular basis, you may want to document it. Take note of the time, date, and other details of the incident. Write down if there is someone else who witnessed the incident. Having some documents to back you up can strengthen your claims if you report to the human resources.

Do not be afraid to report a coworker to the human resources people. If what you are saying is accurate and you have enough information or documentation to back you up, then there is nothing to worry about. Companies do not tolerate bullying behaviors because these can sabotage business success.

Chapter 10: A Quick And Easy 5 Minute Routine To Give You Inner Peace Before Confronting Mean People

Inner peace allows you to heal on so many different levels. It also makes a significant difference in your life. If you achieve inner peace before you confront anyone who is mean to you, you will be much more effective in what you say and do. You will be more reasonable and you will see the bigger picture. It does not take a lot of time to achieve inner peace. You can actually have it within just five minutes.

First, you need to visualize. Close your eyes and let go of all the stress that you feel. Allow your mind and body to connect with each other. Your mind may be filled with numerous thoughts. Gather all these thoughts and keep them at the back of your mind. When you start to focus on a blank slate, your mind slows down and your body relaxes.

Focus intensely on this blank slate or whatever you want to focus on for a while. You can also focus on your surroundings. Notice how the sun shines brightly or how the waves touch the shore. Listen to the different sounds of nature. Listen to the chirping of the birds, the rustling of leaves, etc.

Then, recite your mantra. A mantra is a word or a phrase that has a spiritual significance for you. It is usually used in meditation to achieve relaxation. Your mantra can be anything. You can get one from a book, the Internet, or create your own. Repeat your mantra over and over until you become one with it.

Stop your mind from having any other thoughts aside from your mantra. This will calm your mind and body. Finally, focus on your body. You can focus on your breathing or your heartbeat, for instance. Observe how you inhale and exhale or listen to your heartbeat. When you focus on these rhythms, your mind slows down naturally.

Eventually, presence and stillness will fill your entire body. You should have this routine whenever you are about to confront someone. It will help you become more rational, calm, and focused. Practicing this routine is also helpful whenever you are stuck in a traffic jam, stranded in an airport, or faced with a difficult situation.

Having inner peace allows you to let go of stress, anxiety, and frustrations so you can be happier and more productive. Having inner peace also lets you appreciate the beauty of life better. Furthermore, it inspires you to help other people achieve their own inner peace and become better people themselves.

Conclusion

Thank you again for purchasing this book on Mean People!

I am extremely excited to pass this information along to you, and I am so happy that you now have read and can hopefully implement these strategies going forward.

I hope this book was able to help you understand why people are mean and how you can deal with them.

The next step is to get started using this information and to hopefully live a happy, peaceful, and more productive life!

Please don't be someone who just reads this information and doesn't apply it, the strategies in this book will only benefit you if you use them!

If you know of anyone else that could benefit from the information presented here please inform them of this book.

Finally, if you enjoyed this book and feel it has added value to your life in any way, please take the time to share your thoughts and post a review on Amazon. It'd be greatly appreciated!

Thank you and good luck!

Preview Of:

<u>Power Rapport Building!</u>

Advanced Power Rapport Building For Greater Influence, Romantic Intimacy, Meeting New Friends, Building Confidence, Persuasion, Networking And Career!

Introduction

I want to thank you and congratulate you for purchasing the book, *"Power Rapport Building: Advanced Power Rapport Building For Greater Influence, Romantic Intimacy, Meeting New Friends, Building Confidence, Persuasion, Networking And Career!"*.

Power Rapport Building for Transforming All Areas of Your Life!

This "Power Rapport Building" book contains proven steps and strategies on how to confidently approach and talk to anyone! Gaining the skill of building rapport will greatly enhance your ability to meet new friends, talk to or meet members of the opposite sex, increase your networking abilities for your professional life, and much more!

By using this book, you will learn basic and advanced strategies in using your charisma to start new and improve existing relationships. You can use these relationships for various life goals like improving your career, building a professional network, or finding the right person to spend the rest of your life with.

Let's start building your network today!

Thanks again for purchasing this book, I hope you enjoy it!

Chapter 1 - How Power Rapport Building Can Transform All Areas of Your Life

Becoming socially intelligent will affect all the aspects of your life. Your career, friendly and romantic relationships, family life and your own self-image will improve after you are done with this book.

Career

The adage "It's not what you know but who you know" is applicable in almost all industries. Regardless of how good you are in your profession, if you are not skilled playing the game of office politics, you will not advance in your career.

Knowing the right people and how to get in touch with them will help you improve your chances in improving your career position. Being able to build relationships even with strangers will widen your network. The people you know may be able to help you in time of need. They may also bring you clients for your profession. For this to happen, you need to show qualities that people approve of.

Learning to build rapport will also help you when dealing with your competition. If you are competing with a colleague for example, being socially aware of the situation will prevent you from taking things personally. It will prevent you from playing dirty because you know that doing so will ultimately hurt your social image and ruin your career.

Relationships

By learning how to build rapport, you will know how to get along with people who are most important to you. You will become more sensitive with the feelings of others. You will also be able to act maturely in stressful situations.

Your partner will be one of the people who will most appreciate your social intelligence. Because you are level-headed when dealing with stressful situations, there will be fewer arguments in your relationship. If arguments do happen, you will have the presence of mind to prevent them from creating permanent damage to your relationship.

People who don't have social skills usually let their emotions run wild when in a confrontation. By learning how to build and maintain rapport, you will know how to act to prevent emotional outbursts from further ruining your relationships.

You will also be able to create connections with people in other communities that you become a member of. If you know how to build connections and its advantages, you will not shy away from social gatherings. Even if you are an introvert, you will know how to behave the right way in the presence of different types of people. In the workplace, this will encourage collaboration while in your family life; it will encourage a happy home atmosphere.

Personal Advantages

There are also a lot of personal advantages to building rapport. Shy people tend to improve their self-esteem when they begin to create relationships with new people. These small improvements become social victories that can improve their confidence.

You will also learn how to plan your social image. Having social intelligence makes you aware of your social image at all times. You always have an idea of people's impression of you. You are aware of how your actions affect your social image and you can strategize on how you can improve it to help you reach your career and personal goals.

All the other advantages mentioned above will contribute to your happiness and self-actualization. If you are in a job that requires constant interaction with people, these improvements will significantly enhance your performance.

Thanks for Previewing My Exciting Book Entitled:

"Power Rapport Building! Advanced Power Rapport Building For Greater Influence, Romantic Intimacy, Meeting New Friends, Building Confidence, Persuasion, Networking And Career!"

To purchase this book, simply go to the Amazon Kindle store and simply search:

"POWER RAPPORT BUILDING"

Then just scroll down until you see my book. You will know it is mine because you will see my name "Ryan Cooper" underneath the title.

Alternatively, you can visit my author page on Amazon to see this book and other work I have done. Thanks so much, and please don't forget your free bonuses

DON'T LEAVE YET! - CHECK OUT YOUR FREE BONUSES BELOW!

Free Bonus Offer: Get Free Access To The PotentialRise.com VIP Newsletter!

Once you enter your email address you will immediately get free access to this awesome newsletter!

But wait, right now if you join now for free you will also get free access to the "LIMITLESS ENERGY" free EBook!

To claim both your FREE VIP NEWSLETTER MEMBERSHIP and your FREE BONUS Ebook on LIMITLESS ENERGY!

Just Go To:

www.PotentialRise.com

Made in United States
North Haven, CT
18 March 2022